Summer with Monika

Published by Whizzard Press
in association with André Deutsch 1978.
105 Great Russell Street, London WC1.

ISBN 233 970347

Printed by ESD Printing & Binding Ltd.
Bound by Hunter Foulis Ltd.

Whizzard Press/André Deutsch

Summer with Monika

by Roger McGough

Illustrated by Peter Blake

For Thelma

1

they say the sun shone now and again
but it was generally cloudy
with far too much rain

they say babies were born
married couples made love
(often with eachother)
and people died
(sometimes violently)

they say it was an average
                    ordinary
                    moderate
                    run of the mill
                    commonorgarden
                    summer
    ... but it wasn't

for i locked a yellowdoor
and i threw away the key
and i spent summer with monika
and monika spent summer with me

1

unlike everybody else
we made friends with the weather . . .
mostdays the sun called
                    and sprawled
allover the place
or the wind blew in
as breezily as ever
and ran its fingers through our hair
but usually
it was the moon that kept us company

somedays we thought about the seaside
and built sandcastles on the blankets
and paddled in the pillows
or swam in the sink
and played with the shoals of dishes

otherdays we went for long walks
around the table
and picnicked on the banks
of the settee
or just sunbathed lazily
in front of the fire
until the shilling set on the horizon

we danced a lot that summer . . .
bosanovaed by the bookcase
or maddisoned instead
hulligullied by the oven
or twisted round the bed

at first we kept birds
in a transistor box
to sing for us
but sadly they died
we being too embraced in eachother
to feed them

but it didn't really matter
because we made lovesongs with our bodies
i became the words
and she put me to music

they say it was just
                like
                anyother
                summer

                . . . but it wasn't

4

for we had love and eachother
and the moon for company
when i spent summer with monika
and

    monika

        spent summer

          withme

2

ten milk bottles standing in the hall
ten milk bottles up against the wall
next door neighbour thinks we're dead
hasnt heard a sound he said
doesn't know weve been in bed
the ten whole days since we were wed

noone knows and noone sees
we lovers doing as we please
but people stop and point at these
ten milk bottles a-turning into cheese

ten milk bottles standing day and night
ten different thicknesses and
different shades of white
persistent carolsingers without a note to utter
silent carolsingers a-turning into butter

now she's run out of passion
and theres not much left in me
so maybe we'll get up
and make a cup of tea
then people can stop wondering
what theyre waiting for
those ten milk bottles a-queuing at our door
those ten milk bottles a-queuing at our door

3

saturdaymorning
time for stretching
and yawning
the languid
heavy lidded
lovemaking
the smile
the kiss
the 'who do you love?'
and then the weekly
confidence trick:
the yoursaying its my
turn to make the tea
and the my getting out
of bed and making it

4

our love will be an epic film
with dancing songs and laughter
the kind in which the lovers meet
and live happy everafter

our love will be a famous play
with lots of bedroom scenes
you are twenty-two you are monika
and only we know what that means

5

when the moon is waiting
for the first bus home
and birds assemble
for morning prayers
in the ticktock blanketness
of our dunlopillolove
you open your secret door
and i tiptoe into your womb
quietly
for fear of waking the alarmclock

6

i have lately learned to swim
and now feel more at home
in the ebb and flow of your slim
rhythmic tide
than in the fullydressed
        couldntcareless
restless world outside

7

take ahold of my mind
and gently but firmly
push it between your thighs
into the warm numbness
of your womb
and there let it remain
safe and inlove
whilst you go about the house
doing your sweet everyday things

8

thistime
let there be no
goodbyes
letsstillbefriends
parting –
issuchsicklysweet –
sorrow

let us holdhands
and think not of tomorrow
but of our dailyselves

for there's love here
such love
as makes unhappiness
appear to have mislaid our address

9

monika
i love you more
than all my redleather waistcoats
and i will never give you away
to the nastyman
who lives at the end of the road

10

if i were a parkkeeper
i would strollacross the summerlawns
of your mind
and with a pointedstick
collect all the memories
which lie about
like empty cigarettepackets

and in a distantcorner
where you could not see
i would burn them in the shade
of your love for me

11

you squeeze my hand and
   cry alittle
you cannot comprehend the
   raggletaggle of living
and think it unfair that
   Death
should be the only one
who knows what he's doing

12

you're afraid of the BIG BAD DARK
which loiters in our room
the night it prowls about the yard
the wind howls in distress
a peepingtom moon at the window
waits for the table to undress

it'll soon be tomorrow
there's nothing to fear
you whisper 'never leave me'
then

    put your

        tongue

           in my ear

13

sometimes at dawn you awake
and naked creep across our orangeroom
and drawing aside
our prettyyellow curtains
gaze at the neatroofed horizon
of our littletown
waiting for the sun
screaming with dull pain
to rise like a spark
from a crematorium chimney

then you pitterpad back to bed
your head aflame with fear
you lie in my arms
and you lie:
'i'm happy here
so happy here'

14

KNOCK KNOCK
shhhhh . . .
dont open it
it can only be . . .

the ENEMY!!

15

somethings got to be done
and done right away
monika dont argue
do as i say

i've put out the milkman
and wound up the maid
its well after midnight
so dont be afraid

yes leave the light on
theres so much to see
now monika fetch the razorblade
and lie next to me

16

you are so very beautiful
i cannot help admiring
your eyes so often sadnessful
and lips so kissinspiring

i think about my being-in-love
and touch the flesh you wear so well
i think about my being-in-love
and wish you were as well
                      as well
and wish you were as well

17

i often have the feeling
that when tidying the flat
you are not thinking
of shoes, newspapers
and trivia like that
but of a skullwhite building
where all the inmates
talk poetry to scrambled eggs
and whistle at operatingtable legs

a home for Incurable Romantics
a place to end my days
you will surely have me committed
i must rise and mend my ways

18

away from you
i feel a great emptiness
a gnawing loneliness

with you
i get that reassuring feeling
of wanting to escape

19

you dont say anything
but your eyes tell me
that my standing naked
to seduce the moon
and my crying because
she walked right past
is sadly symptomatic
of a fatal attack of
'push your icy fingers
into my brain
its so hot and lonely here'

20

when the hadtohappen time came
and you quit our hadbeenhappy bed
you pulled the blankets o'er my head
and left me on my sadandlonely own

now i listen darkly to the memory of your smell
and wonder when the sun will melt the storm
our love is like a kitten in a well
the death of something young and softlywarm
the death of something of uncertainform

21

last sundaymorning
when holypictures
fluttered
on dusty church floors
when dockers snored
and mams went heavy
on the gravy browning

you got out of bed
and picking up a hatchet
whose name was
'iloveyoubutwecantgo
onlikethis'
you murdered me
brutifully
then with my tears
still singing
on your hands
you went to your mothers
for telly and a liedown

22

you are a woman of many faces
and the one that suits you best
i fear
is the one you wear when i'm not here
for when you wear your marriage face
boredom lounges round the place

23

you should never have said that
now
your smiles are whiteelephants
and your face a photograph
to be comeacross
some slow brown sunday

you should never have said that
your tongue is a mother without pity
now
love is gone
andanonymous
like the death of a bird in a city

24

we endure cold days and nights
    out on the moors
though we dont like the
    countryside at all

but by spending all our time
    out of doors
we dont have to see the
    writing on the wall

25

monika your soups getting cold
its cream of chicken too
why are you looking at me like that
why have your lips turned blue?

we simply cant go on like this
fighting tooth and nail
why are you looking at me like that
why has your face grown pale?

youre enough to drive a man insane
go completely off his head
why are you looking at me like that
why has your dress gone red?

the only thing i'm sorry about
is that we came to blows
why are you looking at me like that
have i got crumbs on my nose?

alright, i'm sorry i hit you so hard
but nexttime do as youre told
why are you looking at me like that
monika your soups getting cold

26

your finger
sadly
has a familiar ring
about it

27

where have the sunshine breakfasts gone?
orange juice and bacon
the morning kiss and toothpastesmile
you seem to have forsaken

now its greasy grimaces
eggs fried stormyside up
burnt threats and curdled anger
tears in a dirty cup

28

you have gone
you say forever,
and i hear nothing
but the clatter of old leaves on stone floors

29

the sky has nothing to say
and the scaffoldings are full of dead birds
the moon has passed away
and the wind has tears in its eyes
now even the policemen have gone home
and scattered like memories old and worn
the litter

    has

        inherited

          the dawn

30

sitting alone
with my bottle of sauce
KNOCK KNOCK
'who's there?'
noone of course

31

once upon a love
we spent our nights
blowing kisses across
the pillow
now we spend them
throwing plates across the kitchen

32

don't think i'm moaning
or trying to protest
but do you really need
another new dress?
why not smile
its cheaper and just as pretty

33

. . . and when Death comes in
with his zip undone
you'll give in
as you've always done . . .

34

lastnight
was your night out
and just before you went
you put your SCOWLS
in a tumbler
halffilled with steradent

(so that they'd keep nice and fresh for me)

35

said i trusted you
spoke too soon
heard of your affair
with the maninthemoon
say its allover
then if you're right
why does he call
at the house everynight?

36

i have a war on my hands
each night i lie awake
and snipe at terrorists
who run naked
through the steamingjungles
of your dreams
i am on your side
but you dont care
you are asleep and unaware
of my futile heroics
my fear is that one night
i might fall asleep
and you will be captured
my sorrow is that you probably wouldn't mind
(why else keep a white flag under the pillow?)

37

once i paid the piper
and called the tune
but one afternoon
returning home
earlier than usual
i found you in bed
with the piper

you called the last waltz
and now i dance sadly
out of your life

.

1-2-3

1-2-3

1-2-3

38

i wanted
my castle in the air
but it vanished
without trace

i wanted
my pie in the sky
but you gave it me
in the face

39

monika who's been eating my porrage
while i've been away
my quaker oats are nearly gone
what have you got to say?

someone's been at my whisky
taken the jaguar keys
and monika, another thing
whose trousers are these?

i love and trust you darling
can't really believe you'd flirt
but there's a strange man under the table
wearing only a shirt

there's someone in the bathroom
someone behind the door
the house is full of naked men
monika! don't you love ME anymore?

40

monika the teathings are taking over!
the cups are as big as bubblecars
they throttle round the room
tinopeners skate on the greasy plates
by the light of the silvery moon
the biscuits are having a knees-up
they're necking in our breadbin
thats jazz you hear from the saltcellars
but they don't let nonmembers in
the eggspoons had our eggs for breakfast
the saucebottle's asleep in our bed
i overheard the knives and forks
'it won't be long' they said
'it won't be long' they said

41

it all started yesterday evening
as i was helping the potatoes
off with their jackets
i heard you making a date
with the kettle
i distinctly
heard you making a date
with the kettle
my kettle

then at midnight
in the halflight
while i was polishing the bluespeckles
in a famous soappowder
i saw you fondling
the fryingpan
i distinctly
saw you fondling the frying
my frying pan

finally at middawn
in the halfnight
while waiting in the coolshadows
beneath the sink
i saw you makinglove
with the gascooker
i distinctly
saw you makinglove
with the gascooker
my gascooker

my mistake was to leapupon you crying
'MONIKA SPARE THE SAUCERS!'
for now i'm alone
you having left me for someone
with a bigger kitchen

42

in october
when winter the lodger the sod
came a-knocking at our door
i set in a store
of biscuits and whisky
you filled the hotwaterbottle with tears
and we went to bed until spring

in april
we arose
warm and smelling of morning
we kissed the sleep from eachothers eyes
and went out into the world

and now summer's here again
regular as the rentman
but our lives are now more ordered more arranged
the kissing wildly carefree times have changed

we nolonger stroll along the beaches of the bed
or snuggle in the longgrass of the carpets
the room nolonger a world for makebelieving in
but a ceiling and four walls that are for living in

we nolonger eat our dinner holding hands
or neck in the backstalls of the television
the room nolonger a place for hideandseeking in
but a container that we use for eatandsleeping in

our love has become
                          as comfortable
as the jeans you lounge about in
as my old green coat

                          as necessary
as the change you get from the milkman
for a five pound note

our love has become
                          as nice
as a cup of tea in bed
                          as simple
as something the baby said

monika

       the sky is blue
       the leaves are green
       the birds are singing
       the bells are ringing
       for me and my gal
       the suns as big as an icecream factory
       and the corn is as high as an elephants'
i could go on for hours about the beautiful
weather we're having but monika
       they dont
       make summers
       like they
       used to . . .